1st Recital Series

PIANO ACCOMPANIMENT

FOR SNARE DRUM

Including works of:
- *James Curnow*
- *Craig Alan*
- *Mike Hannickel*
- *Timothy Johnson*
- *Ann Lindsay*

Solos for Beginning
through Early Intermediate
level musicians

CURNOW®
MUSIC

EXCLUSIVELY DISTRIBUTED BY

HAL•LEONARD®
CORPORATION

7777 W. BLUEMOUND RD. P.O. BOX 13819 MILWAUKEE, WI 53213

Edition Number: CMP 0858.03

1st Recital Series
Solos for Beginning through Early Intermediate level musicians
Piano Accompaniment for Snare Drum

ISBN: 90-431-1923-7

Foreword

High quality solo/recital literature that is appropriate for performers playing at the Beginner through Early Intermediate skill evels is finally here! Each of the **1st RECITAL SERIES** books is loaded with exciting and varied solo pieces that have been masterfully composed or arranged for your instrument.

Included with the solo book there is a professionally recorded CD that demonstrates each piece. Use these examples to help develop proper performance practices. There is also a recording of the accompaniment alone that can be used for performance (and rehearsal) when a live accompanist is not available. A separate solo Snare Drum book is available [edition nr. CMP 0851.03].

Table of Contents

1. PATHFINDER

Mike Hannickel (ASCAP)

TRIANGLE
TAMBOURINE
SNARE DRUM

2. MULTIPLES OF THREE
(For Triangle, Tambourine, and Snare Drum)

James Curnow (ASCAP)

Edvard Grieg
3. NORWEGIAN DANCE
Opus 35, No. 2

James Curnow (ASCAP)

SNARE DRUM
TRIANGLE

4. RUDIMENTAL RHUMBA

SNARE DRUM

Craig Alan (ASCAP)

5. REGIMENT OF THE RUDIMENTS

Timothy Johnson (ASCAP)

Copyright © 2003 by **Curnow Music Press, Inc.**

6. TURKISH MARCH

Ann Lindsay (ASCAP)

SNARE DRUM

Gioacchino Rossini

7. WILLIAM TELL OVERTURE

SNARE DRUM
Triangle

Arr. James Curnow (ASCAP)

8. THE GIRL I LEFT BEHIND ME

Mike Hannickel
(ASCAP)

9. DRUMMED OUT

18th Century Rogue's March

Arr. **James Curnow** (ASCAP)

SNARE DRUM
Triangle
Susp. Cymbal

Gioacchino Rossini
10. THE BARBER OF SEVILLE
Theme from The Overture

Craig Alan (ASCAP)

SNARE DRUM

11. PARAMETERS

SNARE DRUM

Mike Hannickel (ASCAP)

PARAMETERS: Pg. 3

46

PERCUSSION "BATTERIE" for One Player
Snare Drum, 2 Tom-toms, Ratchet
Suspended cymbal, Flexatone,
Cowbell, Woodblock, Castanets (sub.Woodblock)
Snare sticks and yarn mallets

Antonin Dvorak
12. HUMORESQUE

Mike Hannickel (ASCAP)

48

Copyright © 2003 by Curnow Music Press, Inc.